2

Mayu Murata

CONTENTS

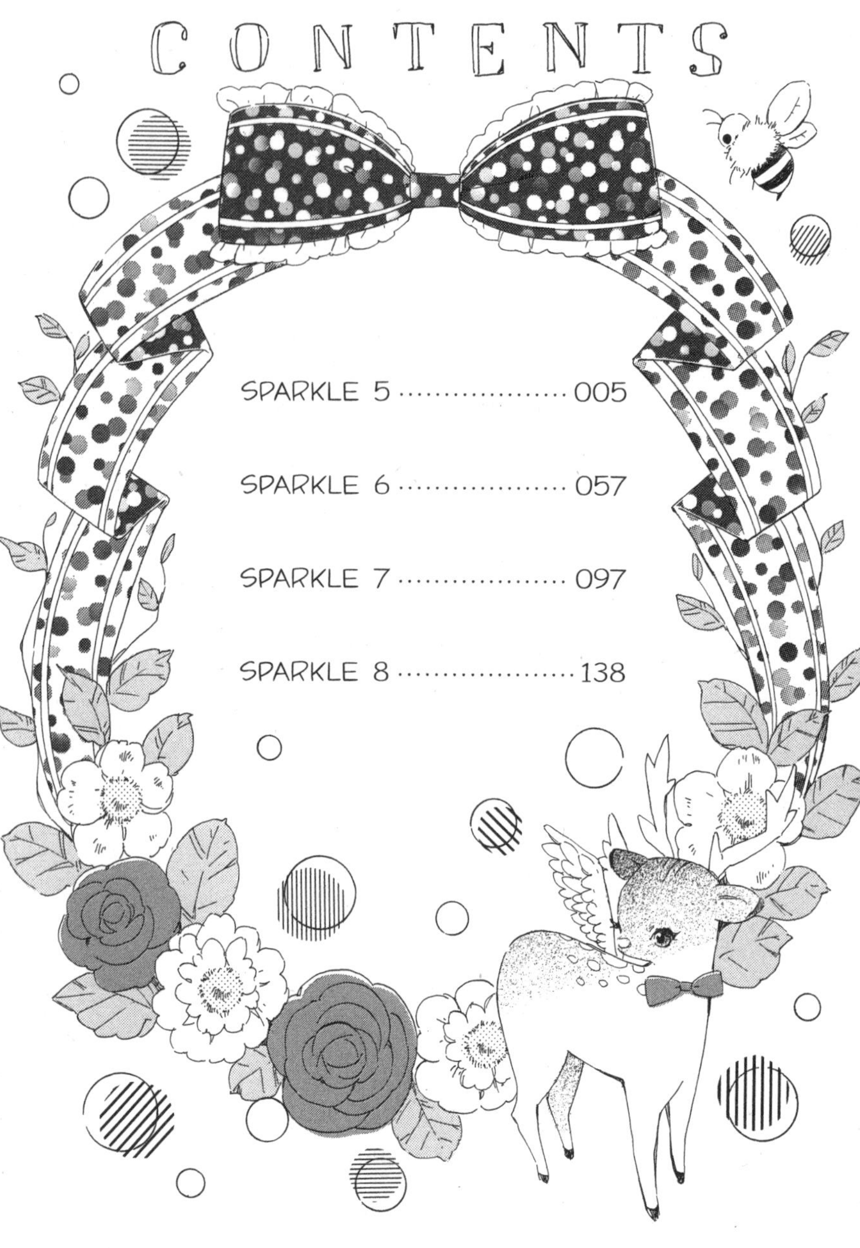

Honey Lemon Soda

CHARACTERS

Uka's classmate. His lemon-colored hair makes him stick out.

High school first-year. Her middle school nickname was "Rocky."

Friends

Satoru Seto

Ayumi Endou

Tomoya Takamine

STORY

In middle school, Uka was bullied to the point that she'd forgotten how to laugh or even cry. But just before her high school entrance exams, a chance encounter with Kai, a boy with lemon-colored hair, gave Uka the courage to change.

Uka's first step is to switch her choice of high school to his instead. Hachimitsu High students all look happy and free-spirited—the polar opposite of Uka's middle school experience and exactly the kind of life she wants to lead. She manages to reunite with Kai, this time as classmates. As Uka strives to connect with others and make friends at this new school, she finds herself receiving his help. Eventually, somewhere along the line, she realizes she fell for him.

When a class seat change puts Uka and Kai together, she sees a new side to him. Uka's feelings for him are quickly growing stronger—but what is she supposed to do with them!?

I NEVER DREAMED...
...I'D FALL IN LOVE.

SMILE!!
HAPPY!!
yeah!!
monSoda

HELLO!!
creed
WOW!
Lemon Soda
Honey Lemon

Mayu Murata presents
Honey Lemon Soda
sparkling love story

HACHIMITSU HIGH SCHOOL—
TODAY IS...
WHAT IN THE WORLD ...?
PFFT!
IS SHE BEING SERIOUS ?
WHO THE HECK...
...IS THAT?
....
SPARKLE 5

...THE INCOMING FIRST-YEARS' WELCOME HIKE.
BUT THIS FIELD TRIP IS BASICALLY A PICNIC!
Dress code: school uniform or tracksuit (Footwear: sneakers)
I THINK THAT'S ISHIMORI-SAN FROM CLASS B.
ISN'T THAT WAY TOO BIG A BAG?
THAT'S MEANT FOR, LIKE, HARD-CORE HIKING, RIGHT...?
PFFT!
HEH HEH!!
I'M THE ONLY ONE... WHO WORE A TRACK-SUIT...
BACKPACK BORROWED FROM DAD
UKA-CHAN!
LOOKING COOL!
I SHOULD HAVE WORN MY TRACKSUIT TOO.
I WENT BACK AND FORTH ON WHAT TO WEAR TILL THE LAST SECOND!
...THANKS...
AN ANGEL...
HUH?

HEY, DID YOU KNOW?
THEY SAY THAT SOMEWHERE ON THIS MOUNTAIN …
…THE TREE CANOPY PARTS IN A WAY WHERE THE SKY LOOKS LIKE A HEART.
OOH… NEVER HEARD OF THAT.
APPARENTLY, IF YOU SEE THE HEART WITH YOUR CRUSH…
…YOUR WISH WILL COME TRUE!
REALLY!?
I WANNA FIND THAT SO BAD!
HEY, AYU. YOU'RE INTO THAT STUFF, RIGHT?
WH— Y— YEAH.
C— COULD IT BE …!?
PSST… UKA-CHAN.
WE SHOULD LOOK FOR IT TOGETHER!
!?
DON'T READ INTO IT.
SATORU'S SUUUPER-DENSE WHEN IT COMES TO ROMANCE.

I—
I'M ROOTING FOR YOU!
THANKS.
SOOO... WHATCHA TALKIN' ABOUT?
ABOUT HOW YOU HAVEN'T CHANGED ONE BIT SINCE WE WERE LITTLE.
OH YEAH?
...STILL...
...SHE'S ON EQUAL FOOTING WITH HER CRUSH.
THAT ALONE MAKES ME JEALOUS.
......
FUI (FWIP)
THE...
THE COLD SHOULDER...
MAKES SENSE. ESPECIALLY TODAY, WHEN I LOOK LIKE THIS...

OH.
SO I'M...

...JEALOUS.
WHAT AM I DOING, GETTING AHEAD OF MYSELF LIKE THAT?

YO, KAI.
WHAT'S UP?
...IS THAT OUTFIT NUTS OR WHAT?

DON'T YOU START MAKING FUN OF HER TOO.
SO MEAN!
I'M NOT.
EVERY DAY...

SHE GETS SO PUMPED UP THAT SHE GOES IN CIRCLES.
I JUST THINK THAT'S SO LIKE HER.
...I FEEL SOMETHING NEW.
HUH, THERE ARE STEEPER PATHS TOO.
BUT TODAY, WE'RE TAKING THE FLATTEST ROUTE...
WOW, WHAT A VARIETY!! AND THERE'S A TON OF THINGS TO SEE, LIKE A TEMPLE AND A BRIDGE!!
MOUNT SOUDA
...SHE GOT SUCKED INTO A PAMPHLET...
WHERE'D SHE EVEN GET THAT?
AH HA HA!
...WHICH MEANS I COULD HAVE WORN THE UNIFORM.
SO, HIKING CLUB! WHICH WAY FROM HERE?

HIKING CLUB...?
KYORO (GLANCE)
KYORO
HACHIMITSU HS
...
THEY MEANT ME!
OH!
WE GO TO THE RIGHT HERE!
AH-HA-HA! SHE ACTUALLY REPLIED!
IT WAS JUST A JOKE.
YOU'RE FUNNY, ISHIMORI-CHAN.
OW!
I JUST BUMPED INTO SOME-THING.
WHAT DIDJA BUMP INTO?
I'M SORR—
WHAT DO YOU THINK?
I DUNNO. PROBABLY A ROCK?
OHHH, A ROCK?
THOSE TOTALLY GET IN THE WAY.
C'MON, ISHIMORI-CHAN!
...I WANT TO DO...

...WHAT I CAN IN THIS CLASS.

...

I CAN FEEL A PRETTY INTENSE STARE...
?
?

...IS THIS ANOTHER WAY OF BEING COLD TO ME?
HE LOOKS MY WAY BUT DOESN'T SAY ANYTHING...

...IF I SAY SOME-THING FIRST...

...WILL HE RESPOND?

WATCH YOUR FOOTING.
IT'S SLIPPERY HERE.
'KAY.

ずるうっ
ZURUU (SLIP)
GYAAAAH!
GASHI (GRAB)
ガシッ
GYAAAAH!!!
WHAT A KLUTZ.
...
Y—
YEAH, WELL...!
...ARGH! DAMN IT!!
AH HA HA!
I BET YOUR HEART SKIPPED A BEAT.
EH, EVERY GIRL GOES THROUGH A KAI PHASE.
UGH!
YOU WIND UP FALLING FOR KAI, AND THEN...
UGH, DON'T!
IT'S POINTLESS TO AIM FOR KAI ANYWAY!!
TOO MUCH COMPETITION!
...BAM! YOU REALIZE HOW HOPELESS IT IS.
YOU KNOW HE'LL NEVER LOVE YOU BACK...

...BUT YOU CAN'T HELP CRUSHING ON HIM ANYWAY, Y'KNOW?
OMG, KAI!!
WILL YOU COME AND GET YOUR HAT ALREADY!?
HFF!
HFF!
HFF!
5 MINUTES AGO
GOT...
...YOUR HAT!!
CATCH ME IF YOU CAN!
JUST KEEP IT.
KAI HAS A TON OF HATS.
YEAH, HE'S BEEN WEARING THEM SINCE MIDDLE SCHOOL.
WHY'D YOU START WEARING HATS AGAIN?
OH!
IT'S BECAUSE OF HIS BED-HEA—
MOGO (COVER)

—DON'T TELL THEM.

!?

!?

YOU'RE THE ONLY ONE WHO KNOWS.

WHY...

...DID HE TELL ME?

...N...

NO... THERE ISN'T A SPECIAL REASON.

THERE ISN'T ...
...BUT...
I KNOW FULL WELL, BUT...
WHAT GIVES...?
...I CAN'T HELP BUT FEEL CLOSER TO HIM NOW.
UKA-CHAAAN!
LET'S EAT LUNCH...
LET'S EAT OVER THERE!
I'M HUNGRY.

WAI— HOLD UP!
CAN I JOIN YOU!?
HUH!?
Y—
YEAH!!

WE'RE EATING LUNCH TOGETHER...
IN THE HABIT OF EATING LUNCH ALONE

PAKA (POP) ぱか

COMPLETELY COLORFUL

I GUESS CUTE PEOPLE EVEN HAVE CUTE LUNCHES...
WHA—
G—
GEEZ, DON'T BE SILLY!!

I'M SURE YOUR LUNCH IS JUST AS...
...CU...
PAKA ぱか
COMPLETELY BROWN (WITH SOME GREEN)

THAT LOOKS LIKE SOMETHING A MONK WOULD EAT.
ALL OF UKA'S FAVES
SO OLD-FASHIONED...

HEY, YOU GUYS.
DO YOU KNOW WHY THE GIRLS KEEP CHECKING OUT THE SKY?

OH, THAT.
IT'S SOME KIND OF...
...GOOD LUCK THING?
THERE'S SOME HOLE BETWEEN THE TREES WHERE THE SKY LOOKS LIKE A HEART.
I'M NOT SEEING ANYTHING.
ME NEITHER.
SAY WHAT?
THERE'S NO WAY THEY'LL FIND IT.
HOW STUPID—

THAT'S THE FACE YOU'RE MAKING...
...KAI.
AM NOT.
ARE TOO.
NAH...
...HE WOULDN'T.

'COS KAI'S...
...GONE TO A ROMANTIC SPOT LIKE THAT WITH A GIRL BEFORE.
...HUH!?
NO WAY. IS THAT TRUE!?
...DON'T TELL THE WHOLE WORLD, SATORU.
YOU'RE NOT DENYING IT!?

NO WAY!!
THAT'S SO OUT OF CHARACTER FOR YOU!!
...WHAT-EVER.
...I SEE.
THAT MAKES SENSE.
THIS IS MIURA-KUN WE'RE TALKING ABOUT.
HE'S PROBABLY...
...HAD A GIRLFRIEND BEFORE.
HE'S BEEN CLOSE TO SOMEONE BEFORE ...
THEN, THE ONE LITTLE SECRET THAT I KNOW...
...IS NO BIG DEAL.

...
I GUESS...
...I HAD THE WRONG IDEA.
HUH?
THE ARROW'S POINTING...
...TO THE ROUGHER PATH...?
WE'RE GOING THAT WAY?
BUT...
HACHIMITSU HS
WHATCHA WAITING FOR, ISHIMORI-CHAN?
THE TEACHERS AND EVERYONE ELSE WENT RIGHT TOO.

...BE OVERTHINKING THINGS.

...IS IT JUST ME...
...OR IS THE PATH GETTING STEEP FAST?
...I KNOW, RIGHT?
I DON'T SEE THE CLASSES IN FRONT OF OR BEHIND US EITHER.
CREEPY.
LOL.
GORO (RUMBLE)
GORO
GORO
HUH!?

SAAA (FSHHH)
NO WAY!
DA (DASH)
GYAAAAH!!
IT'S RAINING!!
AH!

WAIT!
STAY WHERE YOU ARE!!
YEAH, BUT...!
IT'S POURING!
I GET THAT.

BUT DON'T RUN OFF!
WE'LL GET SEPARATED!
UH...
WHAT'S WITH THE SERIOUS VOICE ALL OF A SUDDEN?
IT'S NOT LIKE WE'RE LOST, SO WHAT'S THE BIG DEAL?
RIGHT...
...ISHIMORI-CHAN?

...I THINK...
...WE MIGHT BE LOST.
SAY THAT AGAIN!?
...
HUH?
YOU'RE KIDDING, RIGHT?
WHAT DO WE—
ZAAAAA (ZSHHH)
IT'S REALLY COMING DOWN!!

ZAAA (ZSHHH)

UGH, THIS SUCKS...

MY CURLS CAME OUT!

WHAT DO WE DO?

MY HAIR WAS ON POINT TODAY TOO!

BWA HA HA!

IT LITERALLY RAINED ON OUR PARADE!

LOL!!

DON'T EVEN.

DO YOU SEE ME LAUGHING?

JUST SHUT UP.

...

WHAT'RE YOU GETTING ALL PISSY FOR?

EVEN THOUGH ISHIMORI-CHAN...

...KEPT STARING AT THAT PAMPHLET...

GET YOUR ACT TOGETHER, ISHIMORI-CHAN!!

HEY, YEAH!

YOU'RE THE SOLE HONOR STUDENT!

YIKES.

YOU'RE BLAMING UKA-CHAN WHEN SHE DIDN'T DO ANYTHING WRONG!?

WOW... DO YOU HEAR YOURSELVES?

B— BUT SHE...

YEAH, WE WERE JUST FOLLOWING THE SIGN.

DID SOMEONE CHANGE IT OR SOMETHING?

HMM? THEN WAS THE SIGN WRONG? IS THAT WHAT HAPPENED?

BUT WHY WOULD IT BE?

WHY WOULD THEY DO THAT!?

BUT LIKE, IF YOU THINK ABOUT IT...

...WE CAN JUST TURN BACK, Y'KNOW.

HE'S RIGHT. LET'S ALL TAKE A SEC AND COOL OUR HEADS.

YEAH, THAT'S TRUE.

IT'S NOT THE END OF THE WORLD.

AH-HA-HA!

SNIFF!

UNGH.

SNIFFLE

I HATE THIS!

I WANNA GO HOME!

SNIFFLE

SNIFFLE

MOOOOM!

WAAAAH!

I'LL GO FIND THE PATH!
HUH?
WAIT A...
ISHIMORI-SAN!
ARGH...
I SWEAR...!
ザァァァ
ZAAAA (ZSHHH)
I'M BEING...
...TOTALLY...
...AND UTTERLY USELESS.
ISHIMORI.
ISHIMORI!

I KNEW...
...SOMETHING WAS OFF...
I KNEW, BUT...!
WHEN I THOUGHT I WANTED TO DO WHAT I COULD...
...WAS IT ALL TALK?
THIS IS AWFUL.
IF I'D...
...HAD MY ACT TOGETHER...
AM I WAY OUT OF MY DEPTH?
I'M DELUDING MYSELF.
WHAT IF...
...WE CAN'T FIND OUR WAY BACK?
I'M...

...STILL
JUST—

...CALM DOWN...
...ISHIMORI.
CALM DOWN.

IT'S GONNA BE FINE.

DON (SHOVE)

どんっ

!

BITAN (SPLAT)

びたんっ

WHAT WAS THAT FOR!?

MIURA-KUN.

WHAT?

MIURA-KUN!!

MOUNT SOUDA MA
① MIKIMA SHRINE
② MAINO SHRINE GATE
③ AYANORI BRIDGE

MOUNT SOUDA MAP

THIS IS...

...ON THE MAP...

...
STAY HERE. DON'T TAKE...
...A SINGLE STEP.
ISHIMORI-CHAAAN!
I'M REALLY SORRY ABOUT EARLIER.
I SHOULDN'T HAVE BLAMED YOU.
I LOW-KEY HATE YOU RIGHT NOW.

WACHOO!
I'M THIRSTY.
YOU SHOULDN'T DRINK RAIN, RIGHT?
HERE—
TAKE THIS.
...TH...
...THANKS.

SHE'S REALLY DOING HER BEST...
...ISN'T SHE?
WHAT'S WITH THESE SURVIVAL SHOW VIBES?
YEAH, AND WITH THE RAIN TOO...
LEMON SODA
HERE.
YOU DON'T HAVE ANY LEFT FOR YOURSELF, RIGHT?
I ALREADY DRANK SOME OF IT, THOUGH.
I CAN'T DRINK AFTER YOU.
IS THIS REALLY THE TIME?
THAT'S TRUE.
BEGGARS CAN'T BE CHOOSERS.

...I SWING BETWEEN CALM...

...AND CONFUSION.

MY MIND'S ALL OVER THE PLACE.

I USED TO BE A STONE...

...BUT NOW...

...HA HA!

OH.

THE EXHAUSTION MUST'VE KNOCKED A SCREW LOOSE.

HE...

...LAUGHED...

I NEVER DREAMED I'D FALL IN LOVE.

I WAS THAT GIRL WHO WAS ALWAYS LOOKING AT THE FLOOR...

HEY, SO...

...DIDJA EVER FIND THAT SKY HEART OR WHATEVER?

THIS IS SO NOT THE TIME.

...

WE CAN'T LOOK UP.

STUPID RAIN!

?

...OH YEAH.

EVERYONE, EYES UP.
LOOK WHAT ISHIMORI FOUND!
HM?
BICHA (SPLIK) BICHA
WHOAAA!!!
WHAT?
AAAAAH!!!
...BUT NOW, EVEN WHEN IT'S RAINING...
OOH!
DOES IT MEAN SOME-THING?
IF YOU SEE IT WITH YOUR CRUSH, YOUR WISH WILL COME TRUE!!
I WISH FOR ALL OF US TO GET BACK WITHOUT ANYONE GETTING HURT.
...I'VE GOT MY EYES ON THE SKY.

GAAAAH!!

ARE YOU KIDS OKAY!?

SORRY THAT I WASN'T ABLE TO LEAD THE CLASS!!

I WAS ON CAMERA DUTY!!

AH-HA-HA! GOOD TO BE BACK!

SORRY. WE GOT LOST FOR A MOMENT THERE!

OH, IS CLASS B BACK?

ISHI-MORI!!

BIKU (FLINCH)

ビクッ

I...

...I'M SORR—

THANKS FOR BRINGING EVERYONE BACK SAFE AND SOUND!!

WITH YOU AND MIURA AROUND, I THOUGHT IT'D BE FINE.
SORRY ABOUT THAT.
WAIT, WHY ME?
WERE THE CLASSES BEHIND US OKAY?
THE TEACHER LEADING THEM REALIZED THE SIGN WAS POINTING THE WRONG WAY.
...
YOU GONNA CRY?
WANT ME TO HIDE 'EM FOR YOU?

THANK YOU VERY MUCH.

ALL RIGHT, FOLKS, TIME TO BOARD THE BUS!

WHAT'S THAT ABOUT?

BLUE SKIES...
...LIGHT AS FAR AS THE EYE CAN SEE...
...A RAINBOW AFTER THE RAIN...
DOSU (WHUMP)
ドス

...AND ME, RIGHT IN THE MIDDLE OF IT ALL—
BLAH...
IT'S TOO NOISY IN THE BACK.
I CAN'T SLEEP BACK THERE.

THAT'S THE SORT OF DELUSION...

...

じっ

JI (STARE)

TON (THUMP)

...I MIGHT JUST START HAVING AGAIN.
PILLOW.
!!?

M—
MIURA-KUN!
KEEP IT DOWN.
NO TALKING.

...YES, SIR.
ZZZ

...WH—
WHAT IN THE WORLD!?
IS THIS REALLY HAPPEN-ING!?
I—
I CAN'T BREATHE.
I MEAN, HE'S LEANING ON ME!!

AH!
I'LL LOOK OUT THE WINDOW!!
GYUIN (FWIP)
ギュインッ

YOU CAN'T HELP CRUSHING ON HIM ANYWAY.

...YEAH.

EVERY GIRL GOES THROUGH A KAI PHASE.

I GET THE SENSE...

...I'LL BE STUCK IN THAT PHASE FOR THE REST OF MY LIFE.

YOU REALIZE HOW HOPELESS IT IS.

HE'LL NEVER LOVE YOU BACK.

I HAVEN'T REACHED THAT STAGE YET, BUT...

...I'M SURE I WILL SOMEDAY.

...BUT FOR NOW, IT DOESN'T MATTER BECAUSE...

AND AFTER I MANAGED TO HOLD THEM IN UNTIL NOW.
THIS IS MIURA-KUN'S FAULT.

...I'M HAPPY.

Mayu Murata presents
Honey Lemon Soda
sparkling love story
Honey

BLUE SKIES...
...A RAINBOW AFTER THE RAIN...
...LIGHT AS FAR AS THE EYE CAN SEE...
I THINK I'LL REMEMBER YESTERDAY...
...FOR THE REST OF MY LIFE.
DAD.

SPARKLE 6

THANKS FOR LETTING ME BORROW YOUR BACKPACK!
SURE THING.
DID YOU HAVE FUN ON YOUR FIELD TRIP?
YES!

WELL, I'M OFF!
SOUNDS LIKE SHE'S HAVING MORE FUN THAN EVER BEFORE.
INSTEAD OF LYING TO MY PARENTS...
...I CAN NOW ANSWER THAT QUESTION WITH "YES" NATURALLY.
I CAN'T WAIT TO GET TO SCHOOL!
I'M SO, SO GLAD...

...THAT I CHOSE THIS SCHOOL.
....
...?
HUH? ISN'T THAT MY DESK...?
PILED HIGH
WH— WHAT'S ON IT?
FLASHBACK
...
TORN TEXTBOOK
THUMB-TACKS
FEAR
AH! ISHIMORI-CHAN!
YOU'RE HERE!
SORRY, WE KINDA BORROWED YOUR DESK.
THE THING IS...

YOU LENT US TOWELS AND GAVE US DRINKS ON THE FIELD TRIP, RIGHT?
...IT WASN'T PLANNED OR ANYTHING, BUT...
...EVERYBODY SHOWED UP WITH SOMETHING THIS MORNING.
THIS IS OUR THANK-YOU GIFT.
POTATO
POTATO
COOKIE
Ishimori-chan Thank you
BUTTER
3 Per Pack
5 Packs
FOR ISHIMORI-CHAN
MILK CARAMEL
For Ishimori-chan
suger kiss
For Ishimori-chan
fruit candy
Thanks, Ishimori-chan
For Ishimori-chan
WILL YOU ACCEPT IT?

...HEY, YOU SURE THIS ISN'T A BIT MUCH...?

YOU THINK SO TOO?

I KINDA NOTICED.

SAME GOES FOR THE TOWELS. IF WE RETURN THEM ALL AT ONCE, IT'LL BE INCONVENIENT FOR HER.

YEAH, THAT'S TRUE.

I- ISHIMORI-CHAN?

UH, SORRY ABOUT THIS.

I LOVE IT!

THANK YOU!

OH!
ISHIMORI-CHAN'S HERE?
HOW'D SHE REACT?
SHE LIKED IT.
DOES ANYBODY HAVE A BIG BAG?
I DO!
OH WOW.
カタ
KATA (CLATTER)

IT'S SO AMAZING.
I'M IN HEAVEN ON A DAILY BASIS.

DON'T LOOK AT ME.
I CAME EMPTY-HANDED.
'COS I DIDN'T BORROW A TOWEL ANYWAY.

SOONER OR LATER...
I DON'T NEED ONE.
...WILL I PAY THE PRICE IN EXCHANGE FOR FEELING THIS WAY?
ISHIMORI-CHAAAN!
C'MERE A SEC.
OKAY!

THE HEART YOU FOUND YESTERDAY...
...GOT THREE HUNDRED RETWEETS!
OMG!!
THAT'S KINDA SCARY.
IF IT WAS MY ACCOUNT, I'D GO PRIVATE. LOL.
?
"GO PRIVATE"? "RETWEETS"?
OH YEAH!
I'M USING THIS AS MY HEADER.
"HEADER"...?
IT SEEMS LIKE IT'D BE GOOD LUCK, AMIRITE?
I CAN'T FOLLOW THE CONVERSATION.
HNGH...
MAYBE I'LL DO THAT TOO.
UMMM, WHERE DID I SAVE IT...?
AH.
HEY, CHECK THIS OUT.
HMM?
OOH, WHAT A LOOKER!

WHO'S THE HOTTIE?
DETAILS, GIRL!
HUH?
WHAT DO YOU MEAN?
THAT'S KAI.
DO YOU HAVE THE ACTUAL BOOK ON YOU!?
NOPE.
DEER IN HEAD-LIGHTS (TAKE TWO)
MIURA-KUUUN!!
DYE YOUR HAIR BACK TO BLACK RIGHT THIS SECOND!!
?
BWA HA HA!
WHAT'S THAT ABOUT?
IS THIS YOUR MIDDLE SCHOOL YEARBOOK PIC!?
YES OR NO!?
YEAH, THAT'S RIGHT.
BRING IT IN!
WHAT? FINE, BUT ONLY IF I GET TO SEE YOUR YEARBOOKS TOO!
I WANNA SEE IT TOO!!
OKAY, LET'S ALL BRING THEM TOMORROW!!

BUT MY PIC ISN'T THE BEST!

SAME HERE.

YEAR-BOOKS...

YOU SHOULD BRING YOURS TOO!

HEY, ISHIMORI-CHAN.

HUH!?

IT'S WHAT WE CALLED HER IN MIDDLE SCHOOL...

...'COS SHE'S ALWAYS SUPER-SLOW AND OUT OF IT...AND HER FACE IS ALWAYS FROZEN LIKE A STONE CARVING.

WE WERE ALL IN ON IT LIKE, "HEY, ROCKY!"

....
OH...!
...S...
SORRY.
WHAT I'M TRYING TO SAY IS, DON'T FORCE YOUR-SELF.
UH ...
SH—
SHE SAID "SORRY," SO...!
UH!
AH!
NO, THAT'S NOT...!
I DIDN'T MEAN IT LIKE THAT!
...I'LL...
...JUST STOP TALKING...
AH-HA-HA!

OKAY.

THANKS.

SORRY.

...THEY WERE NICE ENOUGH TO INCLUDE ME, MY PAST REARED ITS UGLY HEAD.
WHERE DID I PUT MY YEARBOOK?
DOSA
DOSA (THUD)
OW!
DOSA
EEP...
AHA!
PART OF ME...
...DIDN'T WANT TO FIND IT.
SURU (SLIDE)
TO TELL THE TRUTH, I'VE NEVER OPENED IT.
I DON'T EVEN KNOW WHAT I LOOK LIKE IN THIS THING.
I FOUND IT!
...
MY MIDDLE SCHOOL YEARBOOK...
PAKA (KRIK)
OPENING JUST A TINY CRACK AT FIRST
EYES HALF-SHUT
FROM A SAFE DISTANCE
...

Uka Ishimori

IT'S SAFE.

AND HERE I'D STEELED MYSELF FOR A REALLY GLOOMY, CRINGEY PHOTO.
WH— WHAT ABOUT ON THE OTHER PAGES!?

CLASS PHOTO
COMMITTEE
GROUP PHOTOS
YES, THEY'RE ALL THE SAME!!
IN NO WAY DO I LOOK LIKE I'M HAVING FUN, BUT I'LL TAKE IT.

PATAN (FMP)
ぱたん
WHAT A RELIEF.
THIS IS DEFINITELY...

I'M SERIOUS, THOUGH. I'M NOT PHOTOGENIC.

WHICH ONE IS YOU?

OOH, YEARBOOKS?

OH, COME ON. YOU LOOK CUTE!

NO WAY!

HEY, DON'T WE KNOW THIS PERSON? FROM CLASS C?

YEAH, THAT'S THEM.

THIS GUY'S HOT.

HIM? HE'S TAKEN.

ARGH!

...I GUESS PEOPLE WHO SPARKLE...

...DO SO FROM THE START.

OOH!

SHE'S MEGA-CUTE!

WHO?

THIS SERINA KANNO CHICK!

Serina Kanno

BUT ANYWAY, KAI'S WAY TOO EXPRESSION-LESS IN ALL OF THESE!

ISN'T THAT NORMAL FOR HIM?

HE DOESN'T SMILE MUCH TO BEGIN WITH.

I LIKE THIS PHOTO FROM OUR CLASS TRIP.

LOOK, IT'S ME!

I'M IN THE BACK, SEE!? THERE!

YOU'RE IN THIS PIC?

THERE'S A GOOD PHOTO OF ME FROM MY CLASS TRIP TOO!

HANG ON, I HAVE ONE FROM SPORTS DAY!

WHAT IS THIS, SHOW-AND-TELL?

I'M ONLY IN...

...THE BARE MINIMUM AMOUNT OF PHOTOS.
BUT THEY...

...AREN'T LIKE ME.

SORRY.
DON'T FORCE YOURSELF.

EVERYONE TIPTOED AROUND MY PAST YESTERDAY.

I'M AN IDIOT FOR ACTUALLY ...
HUH?

... BRING-ING MINE.

ISHIMORI-CHAN?

WHY DID I EVER THINK...

'SUP, KAI!

...I COULD JOIN IN, EVEN FOR A BIT?

I'M SO EMBAR-RASSED OF MYSELF.

TON (TAP)

Graduation

I'M LOCKING THIS YEARBOOK AWAY AGAIN AS SOON AS I GET HOME.
MY PAST...
...EVEN MAKES OTHER PEOPLE CRINGE...
IF ONLY...
...I COULD LOCK IT ALL AWAY...
...AND PRETEND AS THOUGH IT NEVER HAPPENED.
...
HYOI (YOINK)
ひょい

PARA (FLIP)
ぱら
PARA
ぱら
MIURA-KUN!!?
WHICH CLASS?
HEY, WAIT A SEC!
WHICH CLASS?
I WAS IN...
...CLASS 4.
PARA
ぱら

...HUH.
YOU LOOK NORMAL.

HERE I THOUGHT YOUR PHOTOS WERE HIDEOUS FOR YOU TO RUN OUT THE DOOR CLUTCHING IT.
EITHER THAT, OR BULLIES HAD SCRIBBLED IN IT.

...IT'S NOT THAT...
THEN WHAT?

... STUFF LIKE SPORTS DAYS ...
...OR CLASS TRIPS...
I DON'T HAVE ANY FUN MEMORIES OF THEM.

...
AND?

"AND" ...?
AND?
SO WHAT?

SO I'LL...
... FORGET MY PAST.
WHY?

WHAT DO YOU MEAN, "WHY"?
DON'T YOU EVER...
...FORGET IT.
YOUR PAST IS WHAT MADE YOU WHO YOU ARE TODAY.
AS FOR WHETHER THAT'S GOOD OR BAD...
...YESTERDAY...

...OUR CLASSMATES MADE IT VERY CLEAR, DIDN'T THEY?

POTATO

FOR ISHIMORI-CHAN

Thanks, Ishimori-chan

CAN I SHOW THIS TO THE OTHERS?

IT'S KINDA FUNNY.

IT'S LIKE A GHOST APPEARED IN THE PHOTO.

...

I'LL SHOW IT TO THEM MYSELF.

...
KASA (CRINKLE)
カサカサ
KASA
?
KASA
カサ...
...ADD ONE MORE TO THE PILE.
...BUT...
...I DIDN'T LEND YOU ANYTHING...
CALL IT A PRIZE FOR EFFORT.

...
THAT'S
RIGHT.
I'M...

...TOTALLY FINE.
SEE YA.
I CAN MAKE MEMORIES FROM HERE ON OUT.
LIKE THE FIELD TRIP.
THAT...

I'LL...
...HEAD BACK TOO.

...IS WHAT I CAN DO HERE.
UKA-CHAN.

GOT A MINUTE?

TAKA-MINE-KUN.
S—
SURE.
?

GO ON, THEN.
...
?

!?
I'M SUPER-SORRY.
DURING THE FIELD TRIP...
...SHE'S THE ONE WHO TURNED THE SIGN.
HUH!?
Y—
YOU...
...DID ...!?
BUT WHY ...?

'COS EVEN THOUGH YOU'RE A LOSER ...
...YOU'RE CLOSER TO KAI THAN ME.
IT TOTALLY PISSED ME OFF.
YOU WOUND UP BEING, LIKE, OUR GUIDE OR SOMETHING.
I FIGURED YOU'D GET BLAMED FOR IT.

BUT NO WORRIES— I'M ALREADY BORED OF MESSING WITH YOU, SOOO.

'KAY, BYYYE.

...SORRY.

NO, IT'S OKAY!!

...SHE'S GOT THE WRONG IDEA...

...ABOUT US BEING CLOSE, THOUGH.

I DON'T THINK SHE DOES.

HUH?

IT'S LIKE I TOLD YOU LAST TIME.

IT'S UNUSUAL FOR KAI TO APPROACH A GIRL RATHER THAN VICE VERSA.

YOU TWO MAY NOT REALIZE IT...

...BUT TO OTHERS, YOU GUYS SEEM PRETTY FRIENDLY.

THAT MEANS...

...OTHER GIRLS WHO FEEL THE WAY SHE DOES COULD COME OUT OF THE WOODWORK.

EVEN THOUGH YOU'RE A LOSER...
IT TOTALLY PISSED ME OFF.
...I HAVE TO WONDER...
...WHAT KIND OF LIFE YOU'D BE LEADING IF YOU'D NEVER MET KAI.
THAT'S —
FOR ALL WE KNOW...
...YOU MIGHT HAVE BEEN EVEN HAPPIER WITHOUT HIM.

...BECAUSE YOU'RE STICKING TOGETHER.

ARE YOU SURE YOU'RE MAKING PROGRESS, UKA-CHAN?
OR IS THE TRUTH THAT...
HAVING KAI AROUND YOU—
...NOTHING'S CHANGED?

IS IT REALLY FOR THE BETTER?
...
HOW...
...AM I SUPPOSED TO REACT TO THAT?
...SHOULD I TAKE HIM AT HIS WORD?
—THAT I...

...MADE THE WRONG CHOICE IN COMING TO THIS SCHOOL?
HFF!
HFF!
HFF!
1-B
KOFF!
KOFF!
KOFF!
...MIURA-KUN...
HEY, KAI!
...YOU KNOW...

DUDE!

IS IT TRUE? IS THIS SERINA KANNO REALLY YOUR EX!?

...CALM DOWN ALREADY.
—I THOUGHT IF I CHASED AFTER YOU...
HE'S NOT DENYING IT!?
...I COULD GET CLOSER TO YOU, EVEN IF I WAS TAKING BABY STEPS.

NO WAY! WHAT'S SHE LOOK LIKE!?

...

DUDE!! SHE'S A CUTIE!!

BUT...

...I GUESS I WAS WRONG.

I'M JUST GOING IN CIRCLES ALONE...

HFF...
...JUST HOW OUT OF REACH YOU ARE.
KOFF!
KOFF!
KOFF!

PIPIPIPI (BEEP)
ピピピピ
PIPIPIPI
ピピピピ
PIPIPIPI
ピピピピ

LET'S SEE NOW.

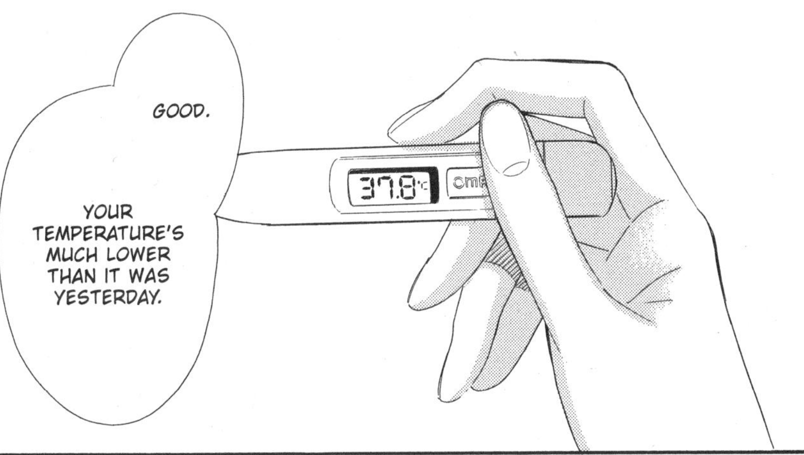
GOOD.
YOUR TEMPERATURE'S MUCH LOWER THAN IT WAS YESTERDAY.
37.8°C

SPARKLE 7

HFF...

I CAUGHT A COLD...

I FELT LIKE IF I STAYED HOME EVEN ONCE...
...MY FACADE WOULD SLIP AND I'D NEVER GO BACK...
MY BACK HURTS...
IT WAS THE ONE THING I WOULDN'T BEND ON.

...
I DIDN'T MISS A DAY OF MIDDLE SCHOOL EITHER.

AND MAKE NO MISTAKE ABOUT IT— MY PARENTS WOULD LET ME GET AWAY WITH THAT.

...WHAT WOULD HAVE HAPPENED...
... IF I'D TOLD MY PARENTS I WAS AN OUTCAST BACK THEN?

WOULD THEY HAVE LODGED A COMPLAINT WITH THE SCHOOL?
OR WOULD WE HAVE MOVED SO THAT I COULD TRANSFER?

HEH!

I COULD SEE EITHER ONE.

...AND THEN, I WOULD NEVER HAVE MET EVERYONE AT HACHIMITSU HIGH.

IN ANY CASE, MY SURROUNDINGS WOULD HAVE CHANGED IN SOME WAY...

HEAL FAST.

IF I'M THE ONLY ONE HOME SICK WITH A COLD...

...I JUST KNOW I'LL MAKE EVERYONE WORRY ABOUT ME.

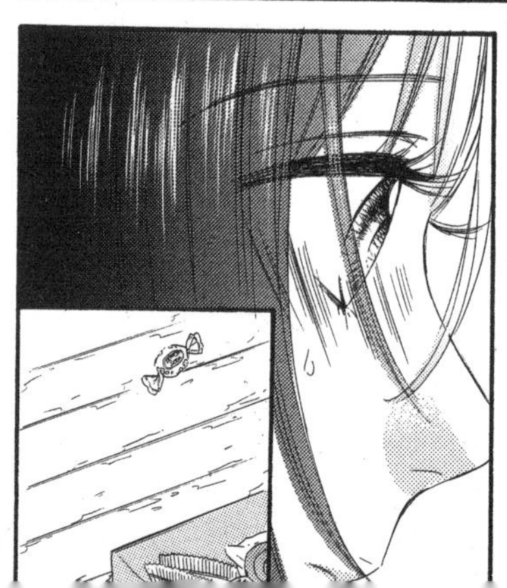

...BECAUSE YOU'RE STICKING TOGETHER.

......

PURURURU (RIIING)

PURURURU

BIKU (JOLT)

DOKI (BADUM)
DOKI
DOKI
DOKI
DOKI
DOKI
DOKI
DOKI
UKAAA!
OH, YOU'RE OUT OF BED?
ARE YOU UP TO TALKING?
YOUR FRIEND'S ON THE PHONE.
PRIOR CALLS FROM "FRIENDS"
SILENCE
...
FREAK!!
GYA HA HA HA!
INSULTS
LAUGHTER IN THE BACKGROUND
...S—
SURE.
I— I'LL TAKE IT...
WHAT!!!!?
HAND OVER...
...THAT PHONE, QUICK!
IT'S YOUR FIRST CALL FROM A FRIEND SINCE YOU STARTED HIGH SCHOOL, ISN'T IT?
IT'S A GIRL NAMED AYUMI-CHAN.

...WHY?
PATAN (SHUT)
パタン
DON'T TALK ON THE PHONE TOO LONG!
WHY WOULD AYUMI-CHAN CALL ME?
KOFF!
KOFF!
HEL—
...
MY VOICE SOUNDS LIKE A MIDDLE-AGED MAN'S!

EH-HRRM!!
H—
HELLO!?
Ayumi-chan!?

LEMON SODA

IT'S ME.

NOPE.

GEEZ!

...Hello?
Ishimori?
...
......
HUH?
!!?
ZA (ZIP)
ZU (ZOOM)
ZA
ZA
ZA
ZA
GATA (CLATTER)
GATA
GATAAN (CRASH)
... WHA ...
... WH- WH- WH...
...WHA...
WHA—!?
THAT VOICE JUST NOW WAS...
...TH...
THAT VOICE WAS ...
...
HELLO?
...M...

Miura-kun?
Yup.
Is that you?
ON THE PHONE, HIS VOICE...
...IS A LITTLE LOW.
IT TICKLES IN MY EAR.
Ayumi...
But that's not gonna happen if you're sick.
YES?
...was wondering what you were doing today.
Says she wants to hang out if you're free.
She got your number from Abe-san.
HANG OUT...!
WHAT!?
UKA-CHAN'S SICK!?

OMIGOSH!
It's 'cos of the field trip, isn't it!?
I'M NOT SICK!
NO...
You totally are.
I AM NOT!
Can you meet us now, then?
...I'M SORRY.
See? Knew you were sick.
THEN AGAIN, IT'D SUCK IF WE CAUGHT YOUR COLD.
MAN, AND AFTER WE CALLED YOU TOO.
...
Uka-chaaan!! Get well soon, okay!?
U—
Um!
...BYE.
YOU'RE ALREADY HANGING UP?

I'M REALLY GLAD I GOT TO TALK TO YOU...
...ON A WEEKEND!!
PLEASE PASS THE MESSAGE ON TO AYUMI-CHAN TOO!!
...
...Hey, Ishimori.
Which way to the station?
HUH?
From your house, I mean.
...FROM MY HOUSE?
...HUH?
YOU GO...
...TO THE RIGHT.
HANG ON. BACK UP.
SHA (SHHHK)
GARA (RATTLE)
BA (DASH)

AH.
OH!
CREATION
LOUIS GARNEAU
AHHHH!
ARE YOU OKAY TO BE UP!?

COME TO SCHOOL TOMORROW!

WE'LL HANG OUT NEXT TIME, OKAY!?
......
YEAH.
YES.

I WILL......!
I MADE A FULL RECOVERY!
WHERE THERE'S A WILL, THERE REALLY IS A WAY!
......

...THERE WAS...
...SOMETHING I WANTED TO DO.
1-B

GOOD MORNING!
AH!
HEY THERE!

UM...
HERE!!
I BROUGHT MINE TOO!
Graduation
...

...I...
...I'M PUTTING THEM IN AN AWKWARD SPOT...
...AREN'T I!?
I KNOW THAT, BUT...

I GUESS THAT WAS...
...PUSHING IT...

THIS FEELS...
...KINDA OFF, YOU KNOW?

YEAH.
I GUESS COMPARED TO EVERYONE ELSE, MY YEARBOOK IS—
'COS YOU...
...SMILE MORE THAN THIS, ISHIMORI-CHAN.
HUH ...?
SHE'S RIGHT.
YOU ALWAYS LOOK LIKE YOU'RE HAVING FUN.
OR IS THAT BECAUSE SHE'S HERE?
MAYBE THAT'S IT.
I BET ANY PHOTOS TAKEN OF YOU AT OUR SCHOOL NOW WOULDN'T TURN OUT LIKE THESE.
HEYYY!

I HAVE CLASSMATES WHO ACCEPT ME...

...

......!
HUH!? IS SHE JUST THE KIND OF PERSON WHO GOES STIFF IN PHOTOS!?

OMG!!
SHE TOTALLY LOOKS LIKE THE GHOST OF A HIKER!!
BWAHA!!
PAA (BEAM)
OH, OKAY! SO SHE'D RATHER WE TEASE HER LIKE THAT?
SO FUNNY, I CAN'T!

CHECK IT OUT.
KAI ISN'T SMILING IN A SINGLE ONE!

HMM?

NO, WAIT A SEC.

HE'S SMILING IN THESE ONES.

HEY, YOU'RE RIGHT.

HUH?

NOT ONLY THAT...

...ISHIMORI-CHAN'S IN ALL OF THEM TOO.

DUDE, NO WAY.
THE POWER OF ISHIMORI-CHAN!

KAI...
...DOES SMILE AT YOU A LOT.

RIGHT?

...
HE DOES ...?
HUH?
YEAH, HE DOES.
YOU DIDN'T REALIZE?

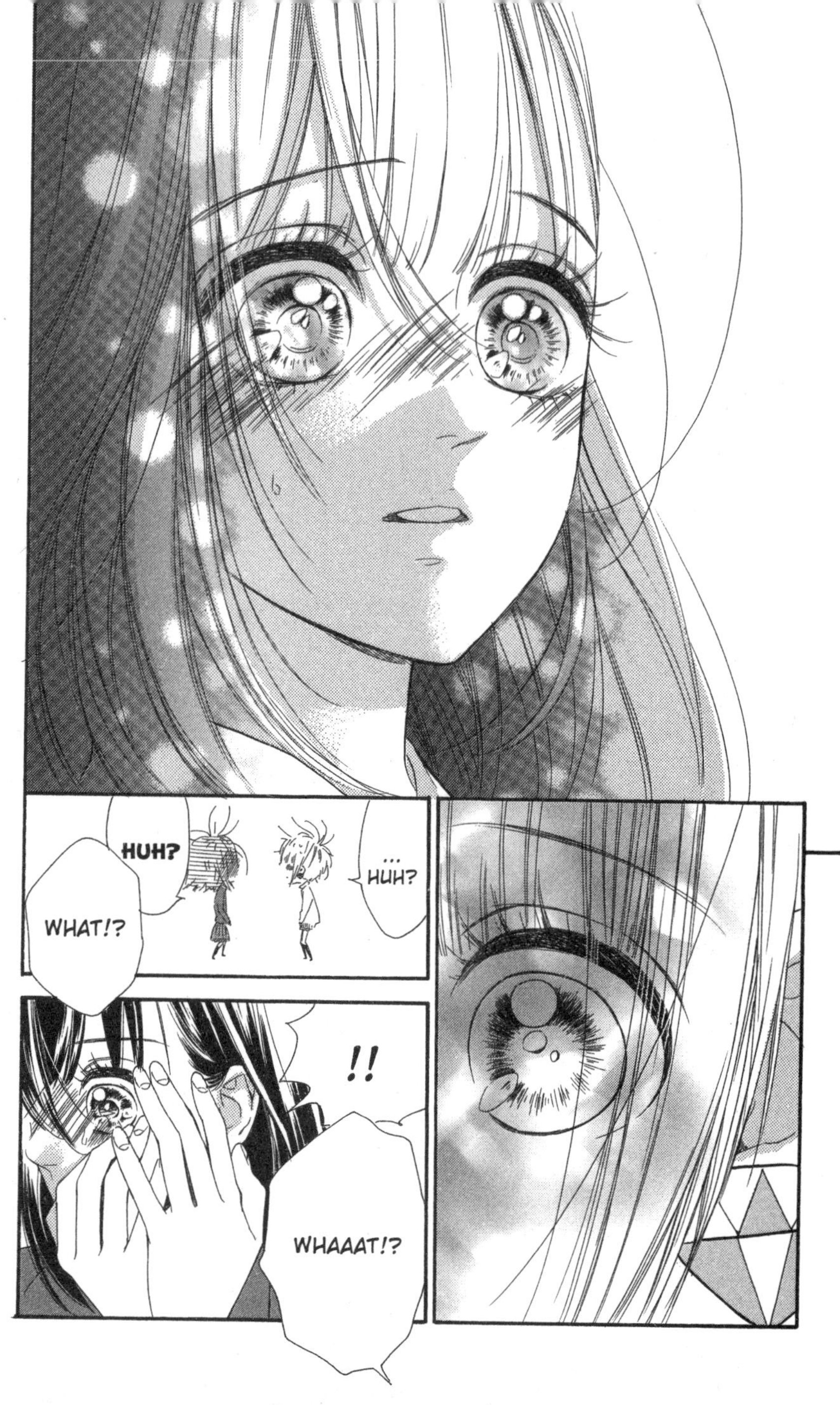

... HUH?
HUH?
WHAT!?
!!
WHAAAT!?

OH.
OHHH.
OKAY.
UKA-CHAN, YOU...
I SEE...
...LIKE...?
...
—OKAY.

I'LL SUPPORT YOU WITH EVERYTHING I'VE GOT!
...
IT MIGHT BE KIND OF AN UPHILL BATTLE, THOUGH...
HEH HEH!
I KNOW!

...A FRIEND WHO TAKES MY FEELINGS SERIOUSLY...

......YES.

THAT'S HOW IT IS FOR ME NOW.

...AND I HAVE...

...A PERSON I LOVE.

...YOU'RE MAKING PROGRESS, UKA-CHAN?

HAVING KAI AROUND YOU—IS IT REALLY FOR THE BETTER?

SHE'S A DIFFERENT PERSON FROM THEN.

SHE'S BETTER OFF STAYING BY MIURA-KUN.

I DOUBTED MYSELF.
BUT MY FINAL ANSWER IS—
YOUR PAST IS WHAT MADE YOU WHO YOU ARE TODAY.
AS FOR WHETHER THAT'S GOOD OR BAD...
...OUR CLASSMATES MADE IT VERY CLEAR, DIDN'T THEY?
NO MATTER WHAT ANYONE SAYS...

...I...
...BELONG HERE.
THERE ARE A LOT OF GOOD SHOTS OF ISHIMORI-CHAN TOO.
...SHE SMILES LIKE SHE'S GONNA MELT.
...MELT...?
IS THAT A COMPLIMENT?
OR A DISS?

...SHE'S CUTE WHEN SHE SMILES.
...!?
WHO'D HAVE THOUGHT KAI OF ALL PEOPLE WOULD COMPLIMENT A GIRL!?
EVEN KNOWING HOW FAR I STILL HAVE TO GO...

...I'M HOLDING ON TIGHT...
...TO THIS...

...MIRACULOUS WORLD.

きーゅ
KYU (SQUEAK)
—THERE!
PHEW!
TIME TO SHIFT GEARS AWAY FROM TEARS!
WAAAH!
BYU (VWOOSH)
KAAN (KLAK)
KOON (KLONK)
!!
PASHI (CATCH)

WHEW!
BATA (TMP)
SORRYYY!
BATA
THAT DIDN'T HIT YOU, DID IT!?

...
IT...
IT DIDN'T.
SO I'LL BRACE MYSELF...
REALLY!?
THAT'S A RELIEF!
THANKS FOR CATCHING MY PHONE!
AH HA HA!
YOU GOTTA BE MORE CAREFUL...
...SERINA!
...TO CATCH...

SEE YOU AROUND!
...WHATEVER CURVEBALLS COME MY WAY.

Mayu Murata presents
Honey Lemon Soda
sparkling love story

WE'VE BEEN BLESSED THIS MORNING.

I CAN'T GET OVER HOW CUTE SHE IS!

NO, SHE'S STRAIGHT-UP GORGEOUS.

QUEEN SERINA!
HEY, GO TALK TO HER.
NO WAY.
I CAN'T DEAL WITH THAT ENTOURAGE OF HERS.
SERINA KANNO-SAN.

A NICE SCENT IS COMING FROM THERE...

BECAUSE OF HER LOOKS, SHE'S BEEN A HOT TOPIC SINCE OUR ENTRANCE CEREMONY...

...OR SO I'VE BEEN TOLD.

I HATE HOW I'M ALWAYS THE LAST ONE TO CATCH ON TO THESE THINGS.

THAT'S WHAT HAPPENS WHEN YOU SPEND LIFE LOOKING DOWN.

I HEARD SHE USED TO DATE MIURA.

FOR REAL!?

SHE'S ALSO...

...BUT THEN...
...WHAT WAS THAT...?
......
I WASN'T SUPPOSED TO SEE THAT. I SHOULD FORGET I EVER DID.
SORRYYY! THAT DIDN'T HIT YOU, DID IT!?
SHE'S A GOOD PERSON...
...MIURA-KUN HAS DATED...
ART
CAMPUS SKETCHING
...AND THE PHOTOS DON'T DO HER BEAUTY JUSTICE.
THAT'S THE SORT OF GIRL...

HOKU (JOY)
ART CLASS IS FUN.
HOKU
DRAWING IS FUN.
LET'S PICK A SPOT ALREADY.
CAN'T WE JUST DRAW HERE?
OH!
WHERE DID UKA-CHAN GET OFF TO!?

HUH!?

I WANTED TO DRAW WITH HER!

HUUUH!!?

AH!

SHE PROLLY STILL HASN'T REALIZED...

...THAT SHE CAN DO THIS STUFF WITH SOMEBODY ELSE.

'COS SHE WAS ALWAYS ALONE BEFORE.

LIKE HOW SHE STARTED EATING ALONE ON THE FIELD TRIP TOO.

...AND GET IT THROUGH HER HEAD THAT THINGS ARE DIFFERENT NOW.
NEXT TIME, LET'S GRAB HER FAST!
...AHH...

I'M GONNA DRAW THIS LADY-BUG.
I LOVE HIM SO MUCH.

...I'LL TEAR THIS OUT AND TAKE IT HOME WITH ME.

IF THEY FOUND OUT I'M SKETCHING THEM IN SECRET, THEY'D BE CREEPED OUT...

KAKI かき...

AH HA HA!

TEE HEE HEE!

...

KAKI (SKRCH) かき KAKI かき KAKI かき KAKI かき KAKI

oooooo

I CAN DO THIS.

1-B

AH! WAIT!

DON'T ERASE THAT...

...YET...

N...

NOOO!

SHA (SWOOSH)

OH! OOPS...

AAAAH!

EVEN THOUGH MIDTERMS ARE RIGHT AROUND THE CORNER...!

I DON'T WANNA FLUNK!

COPYING IT FROM THE BLACKBOARD DOESN'T MEAN YOU UNDERSTAND IT.

THAT'S RICH COMING FROM YOU, SATORU!

I HATE MATH.

WAH!

I'M OUT. PEACE.

UKA-CHAN, WHEN DID YOU GET HERE?

YOU CAN COPY MY NOTES.

OH.

ALSO...

...IF IT'S OKAY...

...YOU WANNA...
...STUDY TOGETHER!?
I—
I MEAN, WOULD YOU LIKE TO!?
I—I WOULD. LIKE TO.
VERY MUCH.
A STUDY SESH?
IN THAT CASE...
...WANNA GO TO A FAMILY RESTAURANT?
I'M HUNGRY.
PAAA (BEAM)
PAAA
LET'S DO IT!
HUH!?

COME ON!
HANG ON!!
ZAWA
ZAWA (CHATTER)
A FOUNTAIN DRINK...
...AND CHICKEN DORIA.
...
WHAT ABOUT YOU, KAI?
GRISTLES.
HERTZ CAR RENTAL
HUUUH...?

I DIDN'T EXPECT MIURA-KUN TO JOIN US...
AND HE'S SITTING RIGHT ACROSS FROM ME...
I'LL GRAB THE DRINKS!
GO FOR IT, UKA-CHAN!
...
THEN I'LL —
NEITHER OF YOU GET UP!!
...
......
SOMETHING TO TALK ABOUT...
OH!
UHHH, UMMM...
"MY FRIED EGG HAD TWO YOLKS TODAY!"
...
WHO CARES...?

I WON'T.

BECAUSE...

CAN WE GET A TABLE?

FOR HOW MANY?

LIKE, ARE YOU BLIND? USE YOUR EYES.

THERE'S A BUNCHA EMPTY SEATS OVER THERE.

SORRY ABOUT THAT.

IT'S FOUR.

TABLE FOR FOUR, GOT IT.

RIGHT THIS WAY, PLEASE.

OH...

...
...SO IT REALLY IS...
FUI (FWIP)
...AWKWARD.
HUH?
HEY, ISN'T THAT SERINA'S EX?
EEEK! TAKAMINE-KUN'S THERE TOOOO! ♡
AWE-SOME!!
LET'S SIT OVER THERE!!
HUH?
HEY!
NIYA
NIYA (SMIRK)
HISO (WHSP)
HISO
...?

HEY, HEY.
MIURA-KUN, YOU DATED SERINA, RIGHT!?
WHO ASKED WHO OUT?
WHY'D YOU BREAK UP??

TELL US!
HEY, HE'S IGNORING US! LOL!!
SO WHY'D THEY BREAK UP??
YOU'RE ASKING ME?

HOW SHOULD I KNOW?
COME ON, YOU CAN TELL US!
I DON'T KNOW THE FIRST THING ABOUT IT.

SORRY, SERINA.
WE'LL CHANGE TABLES.
THEN WE WILL TOOOO.
...

SHOULD WE GO SOME-WHERE ELSE?
NO, THAT'D TAKE TOO LONG...
...FOR UKA-CHAN...

DO YOU HAVE OTHER PLANS?
MY CURFEW IS AT FIVE, SO...
A FIVE O'CLOCK CURFEW !?
PFFFFFT!
OH! EM! GEE!
KYA HA HA!
NO WAAAY !!
HOW SHELTERED ARE YOU!?
WHAT ARE YOU, A WIDDLE KID?
HEY, KNOCK IT OFF.
ANYWAY, WHO'RE YOU!?
DUNNO. NEVER SEEN HER BEFORE.
IT'S A NERRRD!
THE 4 BURGER KINGS
BUT LIKE...
...COULD SHE BE ANY MORE OF A SORE THUMB!?
I THOUGHT THE SAME THING!!
YEAH, SHE STICKS OUT SOOOO MUCH!
LIKE, GET A CLUE, GIRL!

I KNOW, RIGHT!?
SHE JUST LOOKS SO SAD—
LMAO!
BASHA (SPLASH)
GATA (SKRK)

I TOLD YOU TO KNOCK IT OFF!

...
WHA—
DAMN.
OOF...
PACHI (CLAP)
ぱち
PACHI
ぱち
PACHI
ぱち
STOP IT!
...
L—
LET'S GET OUT OF HERE.
SCREW THIS!
PATA (STOMP)
パタ
PATA
パタ
PATA
パタ
...

THAT ...
...WAS SOOO CATHARTIC ...!
SAME FOR ME!!
I'VE BEEN SO TICKED OFF!
THEY WON'T SHUT UP DURING CLASS, AND THEY'RE NASTY TRASH-TALKERS TOO!!
SERIOUSLY, I WARNED THEM A BUNCH OF TIMES BEFORE!
BUT THEY ALWAYS LAUGHED IT OFF LIKE SOME JOKE!!
WELL, IT'S NOT FUNNY!!

NO, I'M THE ONE WHO'S SORRY.

REALLY, I MEAN IT.

DON'T LET THEM GET TO YOU.

WHY...

IT'S UKA-CHAN, RIGHT?
WE SHOULD CHAT AGAIN SOMETIME.
SERINA HASN'T CHANGED.
YEAH. Y'KNOW, IT'D BEEN A WHILE.
YEAH.

KANNO-SAN...
IS THERE ANYONE WHO WOULDN'T FALL FOR HER?
I SHOULD HAVE...
...GIVEN HER A BETTER THANK-YOU.
BUT I WAS FLOORED BY HER.
SHE STOOD UP FOR ME, A STRANGER.
SHE WAS SO COOL.
—KANNO-SAN...

...REMINDS ME OF MIURA-KUN.
BASHA (SPLASH)

THAT'S FOR YESTERDAY.
LIKE, WHO DO YOU THINK YOU ARE?
ZAWA (MURMUR)
WHAT'S GOING ON!?
A FALLING-OUT!?
ZAWA
YOU DO REALIZE WE'RE THE ONES LETTING YOU JOIN OUR GROUP, RIIIGHT?
TEACHER!
OOH, WHO IS IT!?
SOME GIRLS FROM CLASS E.
...I NEVER "JOINED" YOUR LITTLE GROUP.
MORE LIKE, EVER SINCE THE START OF THE SCHOOL YEAR...

...SINCE I'M POPULAR WITH THE BOYS...
...AREN'T YOU THE ONES WHO'VE BEEN FOLLOWING ME AROUND HOPING TO GET MY CRUMBS?
SHE KNOWS!?
WHA—
HYU (WHOOSH)
...SCREW YOU.
GO HANG OUT WITH THAT LOSER ISHIMORI FOR ALL WE CARE!!

BACHIIN
(THWAK)

U—
UKA-CHAN!?
DON'T WORRY.
I'M USED TO IT.
UH...
WHY...?
KURU (WHIRL)
THIS WAS ORIGINALLY ABOUT MY FIVE O'CLOCK CURFEW!
ALL KANNO-SAN DID WAS STAND UP FOR ME!!
IF YOU HAVE A PROBLEM, YOU CAN TAKE IT UP WITH ME!!

GO ON!
BY ALL MEANS!!
LAY IT ON ME!!
WAIT A...
GUI (PULL)
ぐい
!
HOW SCARY.
EASY, TIGER.
YOU MADE "THAT LOSER ISHIMORI" MAD AT YOU.
"GET A CLUE."
"SHE JUST LOOKS SO SAD."

ALL RIGHT, ALL RIGHT, WHAT'S GOING ON HERE?
THIS SUCKS! WHAT A PAIN!
WHY'D THINGS TURN OUT LIKE THIS!?
YOU TOOK THE WORDS RIGHT OUT OF MY MOUTH.
GIVE ME A BREAK!

...SERINA.

...H—
HEY!
!?
I DON'T NEED THIS!
KAI!
EXCUSE ME!!
...
OH GREAT, HERE WE GO AGAIN WITH YOUR STRONG AND SILENT ACT!

NO, SERIOUSLY, COME ON!

KAIII!!

...ASK ANYTHING.

I WON'T ASK ANYTHING.

BECAUSE...

I WONDER WHY THEY BROKE UP?

I DON'T KNOW THE FIRST THING ABOUT IT.

THAT TOPIC MUST BE OFF-LIMITS...

WHAT?
...ISN'T SOMEONE LIKE ME.
WHAT DO YOU MEAN, "WHAT"?
HONEY LEMON SODA VOL. 2 / END

Mayu Murata presents
Honey Lemon Soda
sparkling love story
EAT ME
full
bloom!!
in
HUG ME
spring

Mayu Murata presents
Honey Lemon Soda
sparkling love story

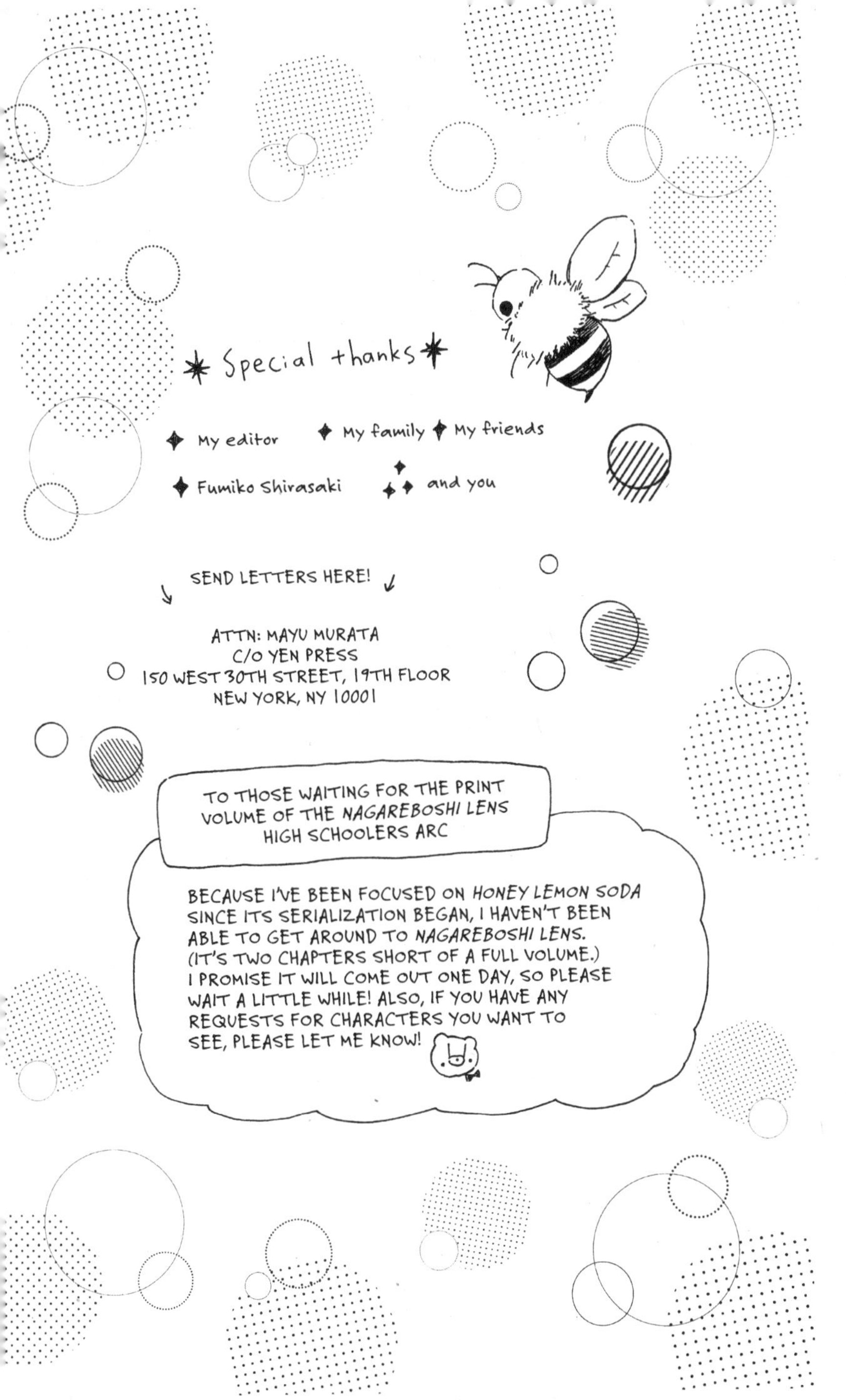
Special thanks
My editor
My family
My friends
Fumiko Shirasaki
and you
SEND LETTERS HERE!
ATTN: MAYU MURATA
C/O YEN PRESS
150 WEST 30TH STREET, 19TH FLOOR
NEW YORK, NY 10001
TO THOSE WAITING FOR THE PRINT VOLUME OF THE *NAGAREBOSHI LENS* HIGH SCHOOLERS ARC
BECAUSE I'VE BEEN FOCUSED ON *HONEY LEMON SODA* SINCE ITS SERIALIZATION BEGAN, I HAVEN'T BEEN ABLE TO GET AROUND TO *NAGAREBOSHI LENS*. (IT'S TWO CHAPTERS SHORT OF A FULL VOLUME.) I PROMISE IT WILL COME OUT ONE DAY, SO PLEASE WAIT A LITTLE WHILE! ALSO, IF YOU HAVE ANY REQUESTS FOR CHARACTERS YOU WANT TO SEE, PLEASE LET ME KNOW!

Honey Lemon Soda

Translation Notes

-san: The Japanese equivalent of Mr./Mrs./Miss. If a situation calls for politeness, this is the fail-safe honorific.
-kun: Used most often when referring to boys, this indicates affection or familiarity. Occasionally used by older men among their peers, but it may also be used by anyone referring to a person of lower standing.
-chan: An affectionate honorific indicating familiarity used mostly in reference to girls; also used in reference to cute persons or animals regardless of gender.
-sensei: A respectful term for teachers, artists, or high-level professionals.

PAGE 082
Ghost: Kai specifically tells Uka that she looks like a *zashiki-warashi* in her photos, which is a mischievous house spirit that is said to look like a child with bobbed black hair.

PAGE 097
Temperature conversion: Uka's temperature is 37.8 degrees Celsius, or 100 degrees Fahrenheit.

PAGE 179
***Nagareboshi Lens*:** This was a manga series that author Mayu Murata published before *Honey Lemon Soda*. It first debuted in 2011 and is complete with ten volumes.

PREVIEW
TO MIURA-KUN, SOMETHING LIKE THAT IS NO BIG
KAI'S EX-GIRLFRIEND SERINA APPEARS...
WE'RE FROM...
...DIFFERENT WORLDS.
AH!
...SENDING UKA INTO CONFUSION!?
DO YOU SAY "I LOVE YOU"...
...AND GET JEALOUS AND STUFF?
...
AS MUCH AS THE NEXT GUY.

Honey Lemon Soda

3

VOLUME 3 COMING SUMMER 2023!!

HORIMIYA ©HERO • OOZ ©Daisuke Hagiwara / SQUARE ENIX
Yen Press
HORIMIYA
VOLUMES 1-16
A sweet "aww"-inspiring tale of school life begins when two similarly dissimilar teenagers discover that there are multiple sides to every story...and person!!!
Visit YENPRESS.COM
TO CHECK OUT THIS TITLE AND MORE!
IN STORES NOW!

HE BREAKS HEARTS, NOT DEADLINES!
MONTHLY GIRLS'
NOZAKI-KUN
IN STORES NOW!
Yen Press
YenPress.com
Monthly Girls' Nozaki-kun © Izumi Tsubaki / SQUARE ENIX

Mayu
Murata

Translation: AMANDA HALEY
Lettering: CHIHO CHRISTIE

Yen Press
150 West 30th Street, 19th Floor
New York, NY 10001

Visit us at yenpress.com · facebook.com/yenpress · twitter.com/yenpress · yenpress.tumblr.com · instagram.com/yenpress

First Yen Press Edition: May 2023
Edited by Yen Press Editorial: Won Young Seo
Designed by Yen Press Design: Jane Sohn

Yen Press is an imprint of Yen Press, LLC.
The Yen Press name and logo are trademarks of Yen Press, LLC.

The publisher is not responsible for websites (or their content) that are not owned by the publisher.

Library of Congress Control Number: 2022946496

ISBNs: 978-1-9753-6333-8 (paperback)
978-1-9753-6334-5 (ebook)

10 9 8 7 6 5 4 3 2 1

LSC-C

Printed in the United States of America